Monique's Moments
Volume 1:
Grief, Healing and Strength

Monique Ross

A devotional series dedicated to healing the inner self and walking in clarity as God gives us revelation.

MONIQUE'S MOMENTS
Volume 1:
Grief, Healing and Strength

Copyright © 2024 by Monique Ross

All rights reserved. No portion of this publication may be reproduced, distributed, or transmitted in any form or by any means, including photocopying, recording, or other electronic or mechanical methods, without the prior written permission of the publisher, except in the case of brief quotations embodied in critical reviews and certain other noncommercial uses permitted by copyright law.

For permission requests, write to the publisher addressed
"ATTN: Permissions" at the following:

Sh'Shares NETWORK, LLC, PO BOX 13202, Jacksonville, FL 32206

Discounts are available on bulk orders by associations and corporations for business, educational, and ministry use. For details, contact the publisher at the address above.

Scripture quotations marked NIV are taken from the Holy Bible, New International Version®, NIV®. Copyright © 1973, 1978, 1984, 2011 by Biblica, Inc.™ Used by permission of Zondervan. All rights reserved worldwide. www.zondervan.comThe "NIV" and "New International Version" are trademarks registered in the United States Patent and Trademark Office by Biblica, Inc.™

Scripture quotations marked MSG are taken from The Message, copyright © 1993, 2002, 2018 by Eugene H. Peterson. Used by permission of NavPress. All rights reserved. Represented by Tyndale House Publishers.

Scripture quotations marked NKJV are taken from the New King James Version®. Copyright © 1982 by Thomas Nelson. Used by permission. All rights reserved.

ISBN: 978-1-942650-64-5
eBook: 978-1-942650-65-2

Printed in the United States of America
First Edition

Contents

Other Books by the Author... iv
Acknowledgments... v
Introduction.. vii

Monique's Moments.. 1
   Moments of Serenity: Seeking Peace During Grief................. 3

Moment One: Grief.. 7
   Endurance in Grief: Life's Most Difficult Challenge............... 9
   Prayer as a Lifeline: Finding Peace in Grief.......................... 15

Moment Two: Healing... 21
   God's Comfort in Our Grief.. 23
   Hope in the Valley.. 27
   Finding Healing in Acceptance... 33
   Live Your Legacy.. 39
   God's Unconditional Love.. 45

Moment Three: Strength... 51
   The Price of Strength... 53
   Strength in the Midst of Tragedy...................................... 59

About the Author.. 67

Other Books by the Author

FUTURE BOOKS IN THE SERIES

Monique's Moments, Volume 2: Confidence and Vision
978-1-942650-66-9
Scheduled: Oct '24

Monique's Moments, Volume 3: Life's Little Lessons
978-1-942650-68-3
Scheduled: Jan '25

PAST BOOKS BY THE AUTHOR

31-Day Grief RESET Workbook: I Will Work for Healing
978-1-942650-63-8
Published: Feb '22

Letters to My Sisters: Pain, Poise, Pride, and God's Promise
978-1-942650-46-1
Published: Dec '20

Acknowledgments

To my family...
    The year 2024 makes seven years for the girls and I being back in Jacksonville. I want to take this time to publicly thank you all for your love and the support that you continue to show us. We could not have been able to settle back in at home so seamlessly without all of your help. As the years go on, we have come to a place of normalcy and moved forward in our lives. But know that no matter how many years pass, we will always be indebted to you all for taking care of us and helping to jump start what would be our new lives.

Introduction

This book has been written to help those facing grief, and most notably, it is dedicated to my "WHOLE HUSBAND" –the one who always saw the best in me.

Rick,

I am forever grateful for you, for your love, provision and your protection for the 21 years we shared with you. Although you are no longer here to see the fruits of your labor, I want you to know you have left a legacy of excellence in service, stewardship and determination. The love I have for you will never be matched. We built a beautiful life for our children together. We miss you more than words can say. You have inspired me to be better as I consider the man you were to so many.

There was once a song we would sing to each other that spoke of endurance and the tenacity it took to be together. So I say to you then, and now, sir, "How 'Bout Us".

– Your Loving Wife

For all the times seeing your face
and hearing your voice pushed me to live, I love you.

Monique's Moments

Moments of Serenity: Seeking Peace During Grief

Welcome to a space where we find ourselves together journeying through moments of healing, reflection, and growth. Here, you'll find encouragement and the reminder that you are not alone in your struggles. Whether you are grieving the loss of a loved one, wrestling with the weight of life's burdens, or simply seeking a deeper connection with God, these moments are for you.

This devotional is designed to guide you through the difficulties of grief and healing. Each entry will offer reflections, stories from my personal moments, and scriptural insights to help you navigate the ups and downs of your grief journey. We will explore the power of acceptance, the importance of remembering, and the beauty of finding strength in vulnerability.

Grief is an unpredictable companion. It appears when we least expect it and challenges popular beliefs about strength and resilience. In this devotional series, we will learn that it is okay if you do not have everything together and figured out, especially as you grieve. Crying is not a sign of weakness; it is a necessary part of the healing process. Throughout this series of books, we will embrace our emotions and allow ourselves to feel. Deeply. We do this all knowing that, through vulnerability, we can find true healing.

Each moment of mine that you read through will be grounded in the wisdom of God's Word. Scriptures placed within these moments of wisdom will offer you comfort and guidance. Anchor verses like Psalm 34:18 which reads, "The Lord is close to the brokenhearted and saves those who are crushed in spirit," will remind us of God's ever-present love and support. Together, we will draw strength from the Bible, finding hope and peace in God's Word of Truth.

Each entry will include moments of prayer and reflection, inviting you to connect with God on a personal level. These prayers will offer a source of comfort and a means of expressing your deepest emotions to the One who understands them fully. Additionally, reflection prompts will encourage you to look inward to develop your awareness of your own emotional and spiritual state while you read about mine.

Because healing is an active process, each entry provides practical steps to help you move forward. Whether it's through creating a remembrance space, journaling your thoughts, or reaching out to loved ones for support, these steps are designed to empower you on your journey. Remember, healing is not a destination but a continuous path of growth and renewal.

Now, please know that you are not alone on this journey. We are not just bodies that remain after loved ones are lost. After loss is when we realize that we are a community of hearts seeking healing and wholeness. So, as you read and reflect, know that others are walking alongside you, sharing in your struggles and triumphs as well as their own. Together, we will support and encourage each other, offering love and comfort as we move through our moments toward greater healing.

PLEASE PRAY ALOUD:

Dear God,
As we embark on this journey of grief, healing and strength, we invite Your presence into our hearts.
Guide us through our grief, comfort us in our sorrow, and help us to embrace the process of healing with open hearts.
May we find strength in our vulnerability and peace in Your eternal love.
Amen.

Moment One: Grief

Endurance in Grief: Embracing Life's Most Difficult Challenge

The journey you have entered into will be long and hard. This battle may involve overcoming the loss of a loved one, coping with the end of a significant relationship, or adjusting to life after a major life change. Whatever it is you will have to decide to stay in the race. You will have to decide to keep moving forward despite the heartache.

You already know that this thing we call "life" is often filled with obstacles that test our strength and our faith, especially when we are grieving. The key to healing lies in our determination to persevere, to trust in God's plan, and to maintain our commitment to the journey ahead. God has a plan for our lives, even in our sorrow.

MONIQUE'S MOMENT:

I have lost many loved ones in my lifetime. I recall the time when I lost my nephew, a son to me. He was very dear to me. My pain and the unending sense of loss were so overwhelming that each day felt like a battle. I held onto Isaiah 40:31 NKJV, which says,

> *"But those who wait on the Lord*
> *Shall renew their strength;*
> *They shall mount up with wings like eagles,*
> *They shall run and not be weary,*
> *They shall walk and not faint."*

This verse became my help as it reminded me that my strength comes from the Lord.

Every day, I *still* choose to stay in the race and trust that God is always leading me toward healing and new beginnings. It wasn't easy then and it's not always easy now, but with faith and perseverance, I find myself growing stronger, more resilient, and closer to God, even in grief.

REFLECTION:

Enduring grief requires a steadfast spirit and unwavering faith. Whether your grief involves healing from the loss of a loved one or adjusting to a new reality without them in some other way, the journey you are on is not easy. However, it is in moments of deep sorrow that we find our greatest strength. No matter how small, each step forward brings us closer to the fulfillment of God's purpose in our lives. Remember, it's not about the speed of your progress but it's about the persistence and faith you exhibit along the way. And this perseverance in grief is not merely about enduring the pain; it's about growing as you journey through it. Every moment of pain we face has the potential to teach us valuable lessons and draw us closer to God. When we choose to stay in the race, we allow God to work in and through us, shaping our character and strengthening our faith. It's crucial to remember that our journey of grief is unique and divinely orchestrated.

What may seem like endless grief could be the journey toward a greater blessing! Trusting in God's perfect plan and timing is essential for finding peace and hope amid grief. Consider the story of Job in the Bible.

Pause.
Take this Moment to Reflect.

Despite losing everything, Job remained faithful. His perseverance eventually led to restoration and blessing beyond measure (Job 42:10-17). Job's story is a powerful reminder that God can turn our grief into joy if we remain steadfast in our faith and commitment to His purpose.

By holding onto faith, staying committed to healing, and leaning on God's promises, you will find the strength to overcome the deepest grief just like Job. Remember, you are not alone. God is with you, guiding and strengthening you through every step of your journey. The journey of grief you are on is shaping you for greater strength and compassion. Each moment of grief is an opportunity to grow stronger and draw closer to God. Embrace the emotion with faith and perseverance, knowing that God is with you every step of the way. Stay in the race, trust in His plan, and watch as He transforms your pain into healing and hope. Keep pressing forward, for the comfort and peace God provides is greater than you can imagine.

A Moment in God's Word:

Isaiah 26:3 NKJV encourages us,

"You will keep him in perfect peace,
Whose mind is stayed on You, Because he trusts in You."

This scripture shares the importance of removing distractions and focusing on Jesus as we navigate our journey of grief. Another comforting scripture is Hebrews 12:1-2 NIV, which states,

"Therefore, since we are surrounded by such a great cloud of witnesses, let us throw off everything that hinders and the sin that so easily entangles. And let us run with perseverance the race marked out for us, fixing our eyes on Jesus, the pioneer and perfecter of faith."

These verses remind us that God is near to us in our grief, offering peace, healing and strength.

PLEASE PRAY ALOUD:

*Lord, grant me the healing and strength
to stay the course in my journey of grief.
Help me to trust in Your timing and purpose,
even when the pain feels unbearable.
Give me the courage to face each day
with faith and determination,
knowing that You are with me every step of the way.
Remind me of Your promises
and let Your word be a light to my path.
Amen.*

TAKE THIS MOMENT FOR YOURSELF:

Reflect on your journey through grief and the challenges you face. Are you mourning the loss of a loved one, or are you trying to find a new normal after a significant change? Take a moment to write down your thoughts and feelings. Meditate on Isaiah 40:31, Hebrews 12:1-2, and Isaiah 26:3. Allow these scriptures to encourage you and remind you that you are not alone. God is with you, strengthening and guiding you through each step of your grief.

LIFE'S LITTLE LESSONS:

1. **Identify Your Grief:**
   Acknowledge the specific loss you are facing. Naming your grief is the first step in addressing it with intentionality and faith.
2. **Find Your Anchor Verse:**
   Choose a scripture that resonates with your current situation. Write it down, memorize it, and let it be your source of strength and encouragement. *NOTE: Many anchor verses will be shared in this book, so find one that resonates with you and hold on to it.*
3. **Commit to Healing:**
   Make a conscious decision to stay in the race. Remind yourself daily that healing is a journey, and each step forward is a victory.
4. **Lean on Your Support System:**
   Reach out to friends, family, or your church or pastor for support and encouragement. Sharing your grief with others can provide the strength and motivation you need to keep going.
5. **Celebrate Small Wins:**
   Recognize and celebrate even the smallest signs of healing. Each step, no matter how small, brings you closer to overcoming your grief.
6. **Pray Continuously:**
   Keep an ongoing relationship with God. Share your battles, fears, and moments of joy with Him. Prayer is a tool that sustains us through the sorrow.

Prayer as a Lifeline: Finding Peace in Grief

Oftentimes, we start the day or week with a list that we rely on to get our daily tasks addressed and completed. *At least that's what I try to do when I'm really on top of things.* For the next lists that we write, let's make sure we include key elements that go beyond simple task completion. We need items on our lists that sustain and uplift us, especially in times of grief and hardship. We must make lists that include prayer in all aspects of our lives—love, grief, work, finances, relationships, situations, and any matters of the heart!!!

    We can take *everything* to God in prayer. Bringing everything to God in prayer is vital in this grief journey especially. We are called to pray without ceasing, but there is a catch. You must have faith to believe that God can do what you asked of Him. You must have willingness to accept that you are worthy of it all. You must have strength to walk boldly, diligently and intentionally into whatever that "thing" is!!!!

REFLECTION:

Now, no matter how hard or regularly you pray, grief has a way of engulfing us. When it does, it makes the future uncertain and the present nearly unbearable. The things that you can actually see are a blur and the things that you cannot see live at the forefront of your mind. Constantly. During these times, prayer becomes not just a comfort but a lifeline.

Pause.
Take this Moment to Reflect.

When I lost my husband at a young age, my world was shattered. The pain was overwhelming, and the path forward seemed impossible to navigate. Yet, I found peace in taking everything to God in prayer. Every tear, every question, every moment of despair, and every decision—I took it *all* to Him.

Scripture tells us in 1 Thessalonians 5:17 KJV to

"Pray Without Ceasing."

This constant communication with God helps us process our grief and find a way through it. But praying isn't enough by itself. We must couple our prayer with faith, as stated in Hebrews 11:6 MSG,

"It's impossible to please God apart from faith.
And why? Because anyone who wants to approach God
must believe both that he exists and that
he cares enough to respond to those who seek him."

This faith empowers us to believe that God can and will provide what we need, even when the world feels like it's falling apart.

MONIQUE'S MOMENT:

One morning, not long after my husband's passing, I recall feeling broken. Very weak and broken. I sat by the window, nursing a glass of coca cola , trying to summon the will to start my day. The weight of loss was suffocating me, and the growing list of tasks seemed absolutely meaningless in the face of death. But I remembered the words of Philippians 4:6-7 MSG,

"Don't fret or worry. Instead of worrying, pray.
Let petitions and praises shape your worries into prayers,
letting God know your concerns.
Before you know it, a sense of God's wholeness,
everything coming together for good,
will come and settle you down.
It's wonderful what happens when Christ
displaces worry at the center of your life."

I prayed right then and there, by the window, laying out my heart before God. I asked for strength. I asked for peace. I simply needed a way to navigate the pain. So, however God was gonna do that, I was here for it! And slowly–slowly, but surely–a sense of rest washed over me, seemingly out of nowhere. Now, it didn't erase the grief, but it gave me the strength I needed to face the day. That day. Just one day at a time. I think about that moment often. It taught me the importance of starting each day with prayer, faith, and the belief that I am worthy of receiving God's love and guidance. That moment reminded me that with God, I have the strength to handle whatever He places before me, even during those times when I feel broken. And weak.

A Moment in God's Word:

James 5:16 KJV says,

"Confess your faults one to another, and pray one for another, that ye may be healed. The effectual fervent prayer of a righteous man availeth much."

In Matthew 21:22 KJV we learn,

"And all things, whatsoever ye shall ask in prayer, believing, ye shall receive."

Psalm 34:17 MSG says something similar:

"Is anyone crying for help? God is listening, ready to rescue you."

These verses remind us of the power of prayer and the importance of faith. They assure us that God hears our cries and responds to our needs, especially in our darkest moments.

Take this Moment for Yourself:

Grief can make it hard to see beyond the pain of the moment, so take this moment for yourself: sit quietly and reflect on God's promises. Remember that you are not alone in your struggles. God is with you, listening to every prayer and comforting your heart. Write down your prayers and any feelings of doubt or fear. Allow yourself to express your emotions freely to God.

PLEASE PRAY ALOUD:

Lord, I come before You with a heart full of grief and pain. Help me to bring all my burdens to You in prayer. Grant me the faith to believe that You can do all that I ask and more. Give me the strength to accept Your love and blessings, and to walk boldly into the future You planned for me. Surround me with Your peace and guide my steps each day. Amen.

LIFE'S LITTLE LESSONS:

1. **Make Prayer a Priority:**
   Start each day with a prayer. Invite God into every aspect of your life. Share your joys, your fears, and your hopes with Him.
2. **Strengthen Your Faith:**
   Remind yourself of God's promises and His faithfulness. Read scriptures that reinforce your belief in His power and love.
3. **Embrace Your Worth:**
   Understand that you are deserving of God's blessings. Walk confidently in the knowledge that He has great plans for you, even when you can't see them.
4. **Act with Intention:**
   As you pray and strengthen your faith, take intentional steps toward healing and growth. Whether it's seeking support, journaling, or simply taking a walk, move forward with purpose.

Grief is a journey, and there will be days when the weight of your loss feels too heavy to bear. In those moments, remember God is with you, guiding you through the storm. By incorporating prayer, faith, and intentional actions into your daily routine, you can find the strength to move forward, one step at a time.

And always, always believe that brighter days are ahead. Trust they will be filled with God's love and His many promises.

Moment Two: Healing

God's Comfort in Our Grief

When you're feeling down and out, in the middle of all things grief-related, it can seem like the world is crushing you. You might feel isolated. You could feel alone and wonder if there's any hope left for you. But hold on! There's a ray of light in all of that darkness. There is a source of comfort that goes beyond anything we can understand. It's the love and presence of God, our keeper, who is always there for us, no matter how bleak things look.

God gets what we're going through. Remember that Jesus has felt every emotion and God knows exactly how much pain we carry and how much we can bear. That's why He's so compassionate, gracious, and understanding when we're grieving. The fact is, grieving is just a part of life. We know that. Still, grief is not something we're meant to stay stuck in forever. Now, it's okay to let yourself feel the pain, but at some point, you've got to open your heart to God's healing. He can comfort and strengthen you in a way that you just can't find anywhere else. Trust me when I tell you!

Because I have certainly tried to find him... somewhere else. More than once. *I know I'm not the only one!!!*

If you, too, have tried searching for God somewhere else, remember that God isn't some distant, out-of-touch being. He's right here with us, ready to wrap us in His loving arms and provide refuge from the storms that come our way. He's always present to help, no matter what we *grow* through. *(Just make sure you're growing in the midst of it all!)*

When you're feeling overwhelmed by grief, remember God's promises. He's always near to the brokenhearted and those who are hurting. Our God will never leave nor abandon us. He's got our backs, and He'll give us the strength and guidance we need to get through tough times of grief. So, if you are grieving right now, don't hesitate to reach out to God. Pray, meditate, or just talk to Him from the heart. You'll find that His presence can lift the weight off your shoulders and give you the peace you truly need.

REFLECTION:

Grief can feel like a heavy burden, but God is with you, even in your darkest moments. He understands your pain and offers His comfort and peace. Allow yourself to grieve, but also open your heart to God's healing presence. He is your refuge and strength, an ever-present help in trouble.

Pause.

Take this Moment to Reflect.

Grief is a profound and often overwhelming emotion that can feel like a heavy burden weighing us down. In these moments of deep sorrow, it is comforting to know that God is with us. He understands our pain intimately and offers comfort and peace to our aching hearts.

Allow yourself the space to grieve. It is equally important to open your heart to God's healing presence. God is our refuge and our strength. Because He is an ever-present help in times of trouble, God is always ready to provide the solace we need.

A Moment in God's Word:

Psalm 46:1 MSG provides reassurance,

> *"God is a safe place to hide,*
> *ready to help when we need him."*

This verse highlights God's compassion and nearness to us in our times of grief.

Another comforting scripture is Matthew 5:4 KJV,

> *"Blessed are they that mourn:*
> *for they shall be comforted."*

These words from Jesus remind us of the promise of comfort in our mourning.

Monique's Moment:

After the loss of a loved one–many loved ones, in fact–I found myself struggling to cope with the overwhelming grief. This was not always because I was down and out, but after experiencing so much loss in my life, I found that I had a hard time letting myself "go there." When grieving, it's normal to feel isolated and overwhelmed by sadness as if no one understands. Yet some of us might understand all too well, and we resist the heavy feelings that grief will bring.

Once I came to this realization, I turned to an anchor scripture, Psalm 34:18, seeking solace in the knowledge that God was close to the brokenhearted *(whether I admitted to myself that I was brokenhearted or not)*. As I prayed and meditated on this scripture, I began to feel a sense of peace and comfort that only God could provide. *Again, without always being willing, able, or aware enough to admit that I was one of those "brokenhearted" souls that the Bible mentions.* This experience of prayer, Bible study and meditation deepened my understanding of God's compassion for His people and His ability to heal even the deepest of unnamed wounds.

PLEASE PRAY ALOUD:

Gracious God,
I come to You with a heavy heart,
seeking Your comfort and peace.
Help me to feel Your presence in my grief
and to trust in Your promise to heal and restore.
Be my shield.
Help me to cope when I don't even have the words.
In Jesus' Name.
Amen.

Hope in the Valley

For anyone experiencing grief that is the result of losing a loved one, I have heard that the second year is worse than the first. Why? Because the first year is unbelievable, but the second year makes the loss final. When you encounter the second year of your loss, you reflect on it sadly. And... you thank God that you made it!!! You think about all the days where you felt weak and broken and tested and tried and alone. Even with all of those feelings trying to take *all* of your attention and change even the best mood, I have something that I want you to take with you in the present year and in the years going forward. It is Psalm 23:4 KJV.

> *"Yea, though I walk through the valley*
> *of the shadow of death, I will fear no evil:*
> *for Thou art with me;*
> *Thy rod and Thy staff, they comfort me."*

    The year of loss brings with it so many unplanned challenges and changes which you are absolutely unprepared for. Along with the loss of your loved one, you suffer many related losses that feel just as profound. When you couple all of these weights together, it compounds into immeasurable grief. Even before the loss, many of us have already walked through deep valleys and felt the heavy weight of sadness and pain due to the cards we were dealt in this life. Yet, even in our valley moments, we have peace in the promise that God is with us. He offers comfort and guidance as we work on acceptance and healing. This journey through grief is not one we walk alone. We have our friends, family, and loved ones helping us through our moments. Still, because we don't always feel that they understand, God remains present as our constant companion.

REFLECTION:

Remember to seek out the comfort and guidance that God provides during our darkest times. Grief is a heavy burden, but the Lord's presence offers peace, healing, and strength. In the years that are marked by loss and resulting uncertainty, be reminded of the enduring promise of God's love and care. Psalm 23:4 is a powerful reminder that even in the valley of the shadow of death, we don't need to fear. For God is with us, and His rod and staff will guide and protect us.

MONIQUE'S MOMENT:

As I reflect on my journey through grief, one particular moment stands out. It was the week I lost my husband. The house felt emptier than ever, and the silence was deafening. I felt a wave of despair wash over me, and it seemed like the darkness would never lift. But then, I remembered Psalm 23:4. I whispered the verse to myself over and over, clinging to each word. In that moment, I felt an overwhelming sense of peace. It was as if God Himself wrapped His arms around me, reassuring me that I was not alone. His comfort was real, and it gave me the strength to face another day.

In another instance, a dear friend called me just to check in. She reminded me of Isaiah 41:10 NKJV. It reads:

"Fear not, for I am with you;
Be not dismayed, for I am your God.
I will strengthen you,
Yes, I will help you,
I will uphold you with My righteous right hand.'"

Her call was a lifeline, a tangible reminder of God's promise to uphold and strengthen me. These experiences have taught me that God's comfort often comes through the loving actions of others and through His Word, which sustains us in our most difficult times.

A Moment in God's Word:

Psalm 23:4 is an anchor verse for anyone walking through grief. It reassures us that God's presence is with us, providing comfort and protection. Additionally, Isaiah 41:10 offers profound encouragement. These verses and others remind us that God's strength and support are always available to us, even in our darkest hours.

In the New Testament, 2 Corinthians 1:3-4 NKJV provides further comfort:

"Blessed be the God and Father of our Lord Jesus Christ,
the Father of mercies and God of all comfort, who
comforts us in all our tribulation, that we
may be able to comfort those who are in any trouble,

*with the comfort with which we ourselves
are comforted by God."*

This passage highlights the reciprocal nature of God's comfort, encouraging us to extend the comfort we have already received to others in their times of grief and need.

PLEASE PRAY ALOUD:

*Dear Lord,
In my deepest moments of sorrow,
I seek Your comforting presence.
Thank You for walking with me through
the valley of the shadow of death.
Help me to feel Your guidance and protection,
even when the path seems uncertain.
Strengthen my heart with Your peace,
and help me to trust in Your promise
to never leave nor forsake me.
Amen.*

TAKE THIS MOMENT FOR YOURSELF:

As you navigate your journey of healing, take a moment to reflect on the moments when you experienced a profound sense of God's presence. Write these moments down in a journal, along with the anchor verses that have brought you comfort. Allow these reflections to remind you of God's unwavering love and support. Consider sharing these reflections with a trusted friend or loved one. Create a space for mutual encouragement and healing.

LIFE'S LITTLE LESSONS:

1. **List Comforting Anchor Verses:**
   Write down Psalm 23:4, Isaiah 41:10, and 2 Corinthians 1:3-4. Place these scriptures where you can see them daily, such as on your mirror, refrigerator, or in your Bible. Reflect on their meaning and allow them to comfort you in moments of sorrow.
2. **Reach Out for Support:**
   Just as my friend called to remind me of God's promises, seek out those who can offer you comfort and encouragement. Don't hesitate to lean on your faith community, friends, or family members during this time.
3. **Offer Comfort to Others:**
   Reflect on how you can even extend God's comfort to others who are also grieving. It might be a phone call, a text, or simply being present. Remember, any comfort you have received from God is a gift you can share with others. *Just don't over do it. Okay?*
4. **Create a Grief Support Routine:**
   Establish a daily or weekly routine that includes prayer, scripture, and reflection. This routine can provide structure and a sense of peace as you navigate your healing journey.
5. **Seek Professional Help as Needed:**
   If your grief feels overwhelming and healing feels impossible, consider seeking the support of a Christian counselor, coach, or grief support group. Professional guidance can offer additional tools and perspectives to help you cope with your loss.

In conclusion, healing is a journey that no one should walk alone. With God's comforting presence and the support of loved ones, we can find strength and hope even in our valley moments. Remember Psalm 23:4 KJV,

"Yea,
though I walk through the valley
of the shadow of death,
I will fear no evil:
for Thou art with me;
Thy rod and Thy staff,
they comfort me."

Let these words be your guide as you navigate the path of healing in the valley, trusting that God is with you every step of the way.

Finding Healing in Acceptance

Grief is *something*, but the initial grief is just the tip of the iceberg. The holidays that you experience after the loss of a loved one are an entirely different weight altogether.

In the days leading up to Thanksgiving in 2018, I found that I wasn't myself. Hmmm... *myself*. Even *that* takes on an entirely different meaning after the loss of your loved one. During that particular holiday season, I found that I was a little heavy. And the truth of the matter is that I was *alot* heavier than normal since a few days before that Thursday even came. I kept thinking to myself, "I thought I had this thing all together." But I have learned. You never know when the pain of losing a loved one will hit you. After losing different loved ones at different times, there were moments when I found myself in tears. In 2018 this happened *a lot*, which is unusual for me because I'm not a crying person. During this season though, I noticed my crying was triggered by the death of a friend's son. Just like I learned that grief will hit whenever it chooses, I also learned that we must be careful thinking we can handle too much. Too much weight can cause you pain, and it will bring you to your stopping point, *which is not always a bad thing*. Here are some questions to assess your weights:

What weights have you suppressed?

What have you tried to forget?

What have you refused to deal with?

What have you unwittingly believed you have conquered only to realize it might actually be conqueuring you?

Monique's Moment:

I vividly recall the morning my tears flowed heavily as I was overcome with the weight of grief. It was an immediate reminder that healing is not a simple or flat process but it is a journey marked by mountains and valley moments. In that moment of vulnerability, I found peace in the memories of my loved ones and the knowledge that I was not alone in my pain. Through tears *and* lots of laughter, I embraced the healing power of acceptance and remembrance.

On this journey of healing, don't deceive yourself into thinking you can fix yourself. Grief is a process! Crying is okay! And *not* being strong is okay, too! Sometimes, you need to break in order to release those things that secretly have you bound. Having the strength to help others doesn't mean you are completely "fixed". Having strength doesn't mean you are not *still* broken and in need of personal help in some areas! *Giving* help doesn't require complete wholeness but *receiving* help does require understanding (and accepting) that you have your own issues! And those issues are just as worthy of addressing as is having the willpower to help others heal. So keep loving on people who are struggling especially during the holiday season. We say only the strong survive, but that's not true. Only the one that endures until the end survives *(Matthew 24:13)*!

As for me, I have been enduring. My love is real, my heart is pure, and my hugs are contagious because of the God in me. It seems like just yesterday when my feet hit the floor that Thanksgiving week and my eyes started… leaking. *lol* But I needed to feel those emotions. I needed to remember my mother, my sister, my uncle, and others. Both my healing, and yours, require acceptance of the loss. Healing requires remembrance of those who we loss. Please stop trying to forget! That can cause you to be forever damaged, so accept the loss. Remember exactly who they were to you and what your loved one brought to your life. Allow yourself to feel. Allow yourself to cry. Then, get up and move!!! Don't sit in dark spaces too long. Heal.

REFLECTION:

When I found myself weighed down by a heavy burden of grief, the pain of losing a loved one hit me unexpectedly. Thinking I had everything under control, I still let my tears flow freely, which was a major difference in my normal way of handling things. This emotional rush had a noticeable trigger point which served as a reminder that grief knows no perfect time to arrive on the scene. Grief can resurface when least expected. This is a lesson in the importance of acknowledging our pain and allowing ourselves to fully experience the process of grief no matter how down we feel.

Pause.
Take this Moment to Reflect.

Grief is a journey that is full of unexpected twists and turns which catch us off guard when we least expect it. We may deceive ourselves into believing we can handle anything that comes our way, only to realize that some burdens are too heavy to bear alone. Suppressing emotions or attempting to forget the pain we feel only serves to prolong our suffering. Instead, we must confront our grief head-on and heart first, allowing ourselves to feel and express the full range of emotions that come with loss.

In summary, here are a few insights on grief and healing:

- Grief is a multifaceted experience.
- Grief encompasses a wide range of emotions, from sadness and anger to acceptance and peace.
- It's okay to not have it all together and to cry as you need to.
- Be willing to admit that we are all broken in certain areas.
- True strength lies in our ability to endure and persevere through the pain.
- Healing comes by leaning on God's grace and the support of others along the way.

A Moment in God's Word:

Read Psalm 34:18 NIV again, which says,

"The Lord is close to the brokenhearted and saves those who are crushed in spirit."

In moments of despair, God is there. He offers comfort to heal our hearts and soothe our souls.

Please Pray Aloud:

Dear God, in the middle of my grief and pain,
I turn to you for comfort and strength.
Help me embrace the journey of healing,
knowing that you are with me every step of the way.
Grant me the courage to accept my losses,
to remember those I have loved and lost,
and to find peace in your presence.
Amen.

Take this Moment for Yourself:

Take a moment to reflect on suppressed emotions or unresolved grief you may carry. Are there losses you have yet to accept or memories you tried to forget? Invite God into those spaces and allow yourself to feel your emotions and process them in healthy ways.

Life's Little Lesson:

Create a sacred space for remembrance and reflection. It could be through journaling, prayer, or spending time by the water. Allow yourself to cry, laugh, and honor the memories of your loved ones. Seek out supportive friends or family members who can walk alongside you on your journey of healing. Remember, healing is a gradual process, but with God's grace, you can find peace and acceptance in the middle of your valley.

Live Your Legacy

When a message came to me that said, "RIP Rick," at the bottom, I got a warm feeling inside and it made me reflect. It was a bittersweet moment and the reflections that followed made me feel oddly happy and safe in my feelings. Now, don't get it twisted, my husband had his flaws and imperfections as we all do. Still, there are noteworthy qualities you can't take away, not even with time. Even as a mostly stoic guy when he was with strangers, Rick's infectious smile—with that gold tooth—and his unwavering dedication to his family left a mark on all who knew him well.

The rest-in-peace message came presenting a sobering moment that really made me think about legacy and the example we leave behind for the next generation. As a woman, I realize that giving birth to children is just the beginning of all they will receive from me. As families and the villages that raise children, we leave enduring impressions on the hearts and minds of our children—sometimes in a way that causes them to follow in our footsteps. This all compelled me to ask myself a number of questions. Questions that I now reserve for you. My questions to you are:

- ❖ Who do you want to be?
- ❖ What will you have done in your life that has helped someone else?
- ❖ Have you used your life to inspire those around you?
- ❖ What example are you leaving for the next generation?
- ❖ What will they remember you for?
- ❖ Do you even care?
- ❖ What will your legacy be?

For me, the weight of these questions served as a reminder that it's never too late to pay attention to the legacy that others receive from us. Our actions, especially in front of children, hold great weight with them and leave a mark on them for years to come. While children don't always seem to be attentive, please know that they are always watching. They are always learning. They are always paying attention, so we've got to pay closer attention to the marks we leave with them now and even after our passing.

Because children absorb and internalize everything, they are the best witnesses for if we lived a good, positive life or not. Their memories will carry the marks of our words, our deeds, and the values we embodied as we lived under their watchful gaze. It's a sobering thought, but also an empowering one.

Let this be a reminder that it's not too late to change the narrative of how they see you! What we do and how we live in front of children matters. They are watching. And they will remember. The legacy we leave behind is not just in material possessions. Our legacy lives on in the hearts of those who knew us. For the sake of our children, I hope we all aspire to be remembered for the love we shared, the noteworthy influence we had, and the positive values we hope to pass along for many generations to come.

Reflection:

- ➢ Legacy is more than just a memory.
- ➢ Legacy is the ongoing influence we have on those who come after us.
- ➢ Every action, word, and decision contributes to the legacy we leave behind.
- ➢ Children, are especially keen observers of our lives.
- ➢ Children watch how we handle challenges, how we treat others, and how we navigate our day-to-day lives.
- ➢ The example we set can shape the values, beliefs, and behaviors of children and others who seek out our example as a blueprint for their own lives.

How does this connect with grief and healing? Well, grieving the loss of a loved one often brings a deeper awareness of and much respect for the legacy they left behind. Sometimes, that legacy is literal. It's the children they left or the business, material possession, financial blessing or even the burdens and debts they leave after passing. In processing our grief about the loss, we use the time to reflect on the life of our loved one, their actions, and the lessons they left behind.

Healing from grief requires acknowledging both the positive and negative aspects of the person's life while understanding that everyone leaves a legacy of some kind.

And every legacy is unique. These types of moments also offer us the opportunity to reflect on our own legacy and make conscious choices to live in a way that positively influences others for the better. All in all, considering legacy makes way for us to *live* well so that we can *leave* well when that time comes.

A Moment in God's Word:

From Proverbs 13:22 NKJV we learn,

> *"A good man leaves an inheritance*
> *to his children's children,*
> *But the wealth of the sinner*
> *is stored up for the righteous."*

This verse highlights the importance of leaving a meaningful legacy that benefits future generations.

In Deuteronomy 6:6-7 MSG says,

> *"Write these commandments*
> *that I've given you today on your hearts.*
> *Get them inside of you*
> *and then get them inside your children.*
> *Talk about them wherever you are,*
> *sitting at home or walking in the street;*
> *talk about them from the time you get up in the morning*
> *to when you fall into bed at night."*

This scripture underscores the significance of teaching and setting an example for the next generation, constantly.

MONIQUE'S MOMENT:

When I received the initial message alerting me about Rick's condition, I was immediately devastated! Yet, over time, the devastation turned into much reflection and contemplation, especially after his passing. I was flooded with memories and despite his off-putting demeanor, Rick had a way of making people feel valued and loved. He was very intentional with his time and resources, often going out of his way to help others quietly. His legacy is one of kindness, sternness and generosity–traits that I strive to emulate sometimes. Reflecting on his life made me realize the importance of consciously working on my legacy and the example I set for my children and those around me.

PLEASE PRAY ALOUD:

Lord,
Help me to live a life that leaves
a positive and lasting legacy.
Give me the wisdom to make choices that reflect
Your love and grace.
Help me to be mindful of the example
I set for the next generation, so that my actions
and words inspire them to live righteously.
Amen.

TAKE THIS MOMENT FOR YOURSELF:

Reflect on the legacy you are creating. Consider the impact of your actions and decisions on those who look up to you. Are you living in a way that you would want to be remembered? It's never too late to start making changes that align with the legacy you want to leave.

LIFE'S LITTLE LESSONS:

1. **Identify Your Values:**
   Write down the values you want to be remembered for. These could include kindness, goodness, faith, or faithfulness.
2. **Live Intentionally:**
   Make choices each day that reflect these values. Show kindness in your interactions, practice integrity in your decisions, and demonstrate generosity in your actions.
3. **Be a Model for Children:**
   Be aware that children are watching and learning from you. Make an effort to model positive behaviors and attitudes.
4. **Reflect and Adjust:**
   Regularly reflect on your actions and their alignment with the legacy you want to leave. Change your behavior as needed to stay true to your values.
5. **Share Stories:**
   Share stories and memories with your family and friends that highlight the values you cherish. This helps to reinforce the importance of living a life that reflects those values.

The legacy we leave is shaped by the choices we make every single day. By living intentionally and reflecting on our actions, we know that the example we set for the next generation is one that inspires and uplifts them. Remember, it's never too late to change the narrative and live a life that leaves a positive and lasting impact.

God's Unconditional Love

In the midst of grief, we often find ourselves reflecting on the lives of those we've lost, pondering their strengths and flaws. Witnessing Rick's passing rocked me to my core. The days, weeks, and months following that were a threat to my joy and they stole my peace. Quickly! Of all the reflections I might have had during that time, I thought often about our marriage and things that I once saw as imperfections. Those traits of Rick's remain unchanging, of course, yet with time, I learned to see his legacy as so much more than the list of imperfections that I held in my mind as his wife. Moments of reflection caused me to view Rick with much more love and consideration after his passing than I would have admitted within myself before his passing. This commentary has nothing to do with Rick per se, but it was my way of keeping a count of the cards I was dealt in life. Good or bad, my habit was to keep count.

Now, I hope we all can admit that I am not the only one who keeps count. But I am willing to be the example that you need to get this thing called life, and love, right. We need to do better! Not because we're depending on people changing or becoming better, but because a person's life is much more valuable than all our tallies of what was right and what was not. Again, this is not an account of whether Rick was a good man. The reality is that Rick was good for ME, honey! MY WHOLE HUSBAND! I knew that before he passed, and I am learning it more and more nowadays.

Rick was good for me and Rick was good to me. Rick was a man's man and he took care of business. He was a man who meant business and I knew, even before I was a military wife, that I was carved out to be the same. I had to be about my business. At a young age, I had to grow up. Quick! Life didn't always afford me the opportunity to be happy-go-lucky or chummy with everybody. On many occasions, I had to look out for myself. I still do, especially with my husband gone. So often, I am called to confront the reality that what is good for us isn't always the thing we rate the highest on the rating scale.

My husband's nature was a good match for me because we married young and his no nonsense disposition set the tone for our lives. Rick was well-respected in his family and that afforded us the opportunity to be a safe place. And that did not mean taking care of everybody, literally or otherwise. Still, sometimes, realities like these can cause your rating to go down with others. These are the things people mark down as our imperfections once they consider our legacies.

I have come to realize that Rick was not as imperfect as I marked him down to be. He was actually very accountable as a matter of fact, so I pray my people are more like him in that way. Be accountable! I also pray my people are not keeping count of my good things and my bad things because what if my good does not outweigh my bad? What if I fall short in the eyes of people? It's not my job to care, but still. What if? Many lives can be touched by the lives that we lead, and still, there will be marks against us because there is no perfection in humanity. There is only perfection in God. To say that another way:

There is no perfection in people, but there is only perfection in God's love.

God's love is unconditional and everlasting. No matter what you've done or where you've been, His love for you remains constant. Cherish God's love and allow it to heal your heart and soul. Let His love be the foundation on which you build your life, knowing that you are loved and valued beyond measure.

REFLECTION:

In summary, here are a few important insights on grief and healing.

- ❖ Grief often makes us reflect.
- ❖ Grief makes us think about our own mortality.
- ❖ Grief makes us think about the mark we will leave on the world.
- ❖ Grief makes us think about the love that we had and the love that we lost.
- ❖ Grief reminds us that our time is limited, we must use our grief and our time wisely to create a positive impact.
- ❖ Healing from grief involves understanding.
- ❖ Flaws don't define us or the people we lose.
- ❖ Reflection allows us to process our perceived flaws and the perceived flaws of others.
- ❖ Reflection allows us to rise above these flaws.

- ❖ Reflection allows us to heal.
- ❖ We can use discussions of our flaws to positively impact and inspire others. That is what truly matters.

TAKE THIS MOMENT FOR YOURSELF:

The love of God is a profound and unchanging truth that we can rely on at all times.

Pause.
Take this Moment to Reflect.

God's love is unconditional and everlasting. It transcends our actions and our circumstances. No matter what we have done or where we have been, God's love finds us! It is *for* us. His love remains steadfast. It never wavers. It never changes. His love allows us to heal from past wounds and build our lives on a solid foundation of healing, acceptance and grace. When we understand that we are loved, cherished and valued beyond measure, it transforms how we view ourselves, our loved ones, and the world around us.

A MOMENT IN GOD'S WORD:

Romans 8:38-39 KJV declares,

"For I am persuaded, that neither death, nor life,
nor angels, nor principalities, nor powers,
nor things present, nor things to come,
Nor height, nor depth, nor any other creature,
shall be able to separate us from the love of God,
which is in Christ Jesus our Lord."

Additionally, Jeremiah 31:3 NIV tells us,

"The Lord appeared to us in the past, saying:
"I have loved you with an everlasting love;
I have drawn you with unfailing kindness.'"

These scriptures remind us of the powerful and unbreakable bond we have with God through His love.

MONIQUE'S MOMENT:

Don't be surprised to know that there have been times when I felt unworthy of God's love due to mistakes I made. Like others, I have been filled with guilt and shame before. I believed I was beyond redemption. During one of these periods, a close friend reminded me of Romans 8:38-39 above. As I meditated on this scripture, I felt God's love wash over me. It was not easy to feel myself worthy of God's love again. However, the more I revisited God's word, I could literally feel my mind changing about my value in God's eyes. This changed my heart and renewed my spirit. It didn't just help me get it together with *me*, but it helped me have grace for others *(and stop keeping count, if you know what I mean). lol* It was a turning point that helped me get to a point where I could *receive* God's unconditional love and get my healing.

And I've had to come back to this same verse time and time again. But now when I read Romans 8:38-39, it's not because I'm wrestling with what it says. It's because I am reinforcing my faith in what I already know:

"For I am persuaded, that neither death, nor life,
nor angels, nor principalities, nor powers,
nor things present, nor things to come,
Nor height, nor depth, nor any other creature,

shall be able to separate us from the love of God, which is in Christ Jesus our Lord."

That is where I find my truth in knowing there is perfection in God's love!

PLEASE PRAY ALOUD:

---

*Lord,
Thank You for Your unconditional and everlasting love.
Help me to receive this love fully
and allow it to heal my heart and soul.
Remind me daily that I am cherished
and loved beyond measure.
Let Your love be the foundation of my life,
guiding me in all that I do.
Amen.*

LIFE'S LITTLE LESSON:

Spend time reflecting on the unconditional love of God. Write down Romans 8:38-39 and Jeremiah 31:3, and meditate on these verses throughout the week. Consider how embracing God's love can transform your life and bring healing. Share this message of love with someone who may need to hear it.

Moment Three: Strength

The Price of Strength

Have you experienced loss?
Have you experienced pain?
Have you experienced hurt?
Have you experienced being alone?
Have you experienced being left behind?
Have you experienced disappointment?
Have you experienced being looked over?
Have you experienced rejection?
Have you experienced sometone's "No"?
Have you experienced "not you" or "not yet"?
Have you experienced not being the one?
Have you ever hurt yourself trying to save yourself?
Do you have what it takes to be strong?

Here is today's life lesson:
There is a Price to Pay for Strength!!

Many people think being strong is fun, glamorous and *easy*. Let me share the facts with you: the price of strength is *expensive* and a lot of us don't have the currency to pay. If you have never seen darkness, how can you help someone else walk in the light? If you haven't experienced self denial, how can you help someone else to walk away from something or someone they love in order to save themselves?

In this strength walk, you have to go through some *heavy* stuff! And I mean HEAVY!!! You have to endure sleepless nights. You have to see life eye-to-eye and tell life, "I see you, but I see God on the other side!" In this strength walk, you can't afford to get sidetracked by what's happening to you or be overcome by what's going on in the lives of those around you. This thing called strength is a WHOLE ENTIRE PROCESS! Physical strength is not what's going to carry you *(although you must take care of your body along the way)*. It is your mental and spiritual strength that is actually going to carry you and keep you.

I believe strength is assigned to some of us by God to be our spiritual gift. *Why*, you ask? Because God allows some of us to keep walking without falling in spite of the circumstance. He allows some of us to keep our minds and not go crazy when it would be perfectly understandable if we did. God allows some of us the capacity to detach from emotion long enough to think clearly and rationally.

Be mindful of these selected people around you who God has given special gifts of strength. He had to carry them through some valleys and over many mountains to build up their strength repository. These folks have often faced tough times to become strong and resilient. They didn't just end up so resolved on their own accord, but it is God's power working in them that strengthens them.

But be not fooled. Even the toughest of us get weak. When strength walkers get weak, we want to quit, we want to give up, we want to stay in bed all day and cry. Sometimes, we just want to have our way, but that's not how life works. Still, deep down–despite our desire to throw in the towel–there's a force inside us that keeps us from giving in to those desires. That force is God. Do you feel it inside of you? That strength that you're pulling on... that's the strength and the grace of God! Now the question is, have you lived a full enough life for your repository to be full enough for you to give some strength to others? If so, do that! God's got your back. And please know that this thing called life will make you or it will break you. At other times, it will make you *and* break you. Just know that you are not alone. God has assigned some people to you who will help carry any baggage that keeps you bound. With their help and the help of God, continue to walk in your purpose. Be of good faith and have courage because whether you think your trials are just or whether you think they are unjust, we *all* gotta go through!

REFLECTION:

After you face loss, pain, disappointment, or rejection, you might have felt alone, left behind, or overwhelmed by life's challenges. Challenges like these might make you wonder what it takes to be strong. Strength isn't just about appearing resilient; it comes with a price. Many think of strength as glamorous, but in reality, it demands sacrifices and endurance. It requires facing darkness, experiencing self-denial, and navigating through life's trials with steadfast, immovable faith.

Pause.
Take this Moment to Reflect.

Remember, we're not talking about the type of strength that is merely about physical prowess. We're talking about the type of strength that is rooted in mental and spiritual resilience. We're talking about confronting life's adversities head-on, even when the road ahead seems daunting. Developing this type of strength requires a process that shapes and molds us through trials and tribulations. And while some may see strength as a personal attribute, I want to remind you once again that strength is ultimately a gift from God, bestowed upon those who trust in His guidance and lean on His power.

This wisdom teaches us that strength is not some one-time achievement. It is a continual evolution that constantly refines our resolve. All of this development teaches us just how to persevere when everything seems like it's about to fall apart.

If you are one who God is developing in His strength, please don't pretend to be invincible–there's no need for it. Strength is less of a burden to you once you learn to acknowledge your vulnerabilities and trust that God will carry you through every trial and tribulation.

A Moment in God's Word:

Philippians 4:13 KJV declares,

> *"I can do all things through Christ which strengtheneth me."*

This verse reminds us that our strength comes from God, enabling us to face any challenge that comes our way.

Please Pray Aloud:

Heavenly Father,
Grant me the strength to endure life's trials
with grace and courage.
Help me to rely on Your power and guidance in times of
weakness, knowing that You are always with me.
Strengthen my faith and fill me with Your peace
as I walk in Your purpose.
Amen.

Take this Moment for Yourself:

Reflect on a time when you felt strong in the midst of adversity. How did God sustain you during that challenging season?

Pause.
Take this Moment to Reflect.

Take a moment to thank Him for His faithfulness and ask Him to continue to strengthen you in times of need.

Life's Little Lesson:

Identify a challenge or trial you are currently facing. Write down Philippians 4:13 and meditate on it daily, reminding yourself that God's strength is sufficient for you. Seek support from trusted friends or mentors who can pray with you and encourage you on your journey of strength and resilience. Remember, you are not alone, and God is always with you, empowering you to overcome every obstacle in your path.

Strength in the Midst of Tragedy

While I reminisced on the morning of June 16, 2020, I was confronted with the painful memories of the day my husband passed away on June 17, 2017, three years earlier. On that morning, I was reminded of a few things. While the date of his passing was quite significant–*obviously*–I found the morning of June 16th in 2020 to be even more difficult.

"Why?" You may ask.

Well, you see, June 16th was the day I got the call. Shannon, my husband's fellow airman, was the one who called to inform me that my life would be forever changed. Shannon was the one who came to my rescue when Rick passed out on the track. Now, I am not sharing this part of my journey to expose the details of that tragic day. I am sharing this to shine a little light on how things we say manifest themselves in our lives and to show you who you are at the core.

Starting back in 2013 and continuing through 2018, the many posts that I shared on my Facebook profile on June 16th each year tell the story of love and pain and strength and heartache and fear and perseverance and faith in GOD. Without even knowing it, on that very day for all those years, I was telling a story that needed to be written in living color. In 2013, I posted a beautiful picture of my family not knowing that it would be our last professional photo as a family–my youngest, Zarah, was in my belly. On that date in 2014, 2015, and 2016, I talked of loss and I spoke words of encouragement for myself and others. In 2017, I posted a "THUG LIFE" birthday shout out to Tupac *(because he was awesome!!!)*. I had no clue that on that very same day, I would have to tap into the toughest, most gangster part of me to get through what was about to happen to my daughters and I. Lastly, one year later, I posted about being there for my best friend at the worst time of her life while I was still figuring out my new life.

The lesson in all of this is that at our best we are loved. At our worst, we can show love, and when we are in those in-between spaces, we can still speak love. No matter what *you* are faced with, there is a part of you that will always speak for you. There is no perfection in people but there is perfection in God's love. One reality in our life as Christians is that it is our job–at every point in life–to make sure we can show God's love to someone else. And I promise you that God will continually keep you and cover you while you are doing this great work that we are all called to do.

Life is not perfect and it's not all sweet, but I know that it is still worth living. I pray you know that, too. When life throws you the best and hardest curve balls that you can imagine, dig deep and hold on tight. Fight to make sure you don't lose who you are based on what you are going through.

Reflecting on these memories, I am reminded of the power of our words and how our actions shape our worlds and reveal our true selves. Despite the love, pain, strength, heartache, fear, perseverance, and faith depicted in my many memories shared on June 16th each yeaer, one constant remains:

God's love and presence is unwavering in the midst of adversity.

MONIQUE'S MOMENT:

Tragedy has a way of revealing our character and the strength of our faith. In moments of loss and despair, we are faced with the choice to succumb to our circumstances or rise above them with courage. As I navigated through the darkest days of grief, I discovered an inner strength and resolve that I never knew I possessed. Just as I had made a practice to love on, encourage, and be there for others, it was imperative that I did these things for myself. Even when I had no energy for displaying or even uttering God's goodness, it was through the support of loved ones that I found the courage to persevere. My friends and family members were simply giving me back what was already given to them.

Still, the journey of grief has proven to be tumultuous and filled with moments of sorrow and despair. Yet, amidst the pain, I experienced moments of profound grace and healing. That family photo that I posted unaware that it would be our last one together before my husband's passing is a moment in our journey that my children and I will cherish forever. Each memory captured in those years of memories tells of love, loss, and the resilience of our united spirits. Despite the pain of losing my husband, I found solace back then because God's love remained constant. That love guided me through the darkest moments of my life.

A Moment in God's Word:

Grief is a complex and deeply personal journey that can leave anyone feeling lost and overwhelmed. However, in the midst of that pain, find comfort in God's unfailing love and presence.

Psalm 147:3 MSG reminds us that

*"He heals the heartbroken
and bandages their wounds."*

Even in our darkest moments, God is there, offering us His strength and grace to endure.

Please Pray Aloud:

*Heavenly Father,
in the midst of our pain and sorrow,
we turn to you for comfort and healing.
Surround us with your love and presence, and grant us
the strength to endure the challenges that lie ahead.
Help us to find hope in the midst of despair and to trust
in your plan for our lives.
Amen.*

Take this Moment for Yourself:

Consider the challenges and trials you have faced in your own life. How have these experiences shaped you?

Pause.
Take this Moment to Reflect.

Consider how God's love has sustained you through difficult times and how you can extend that love to others who are struggling.

LIFE'S LITTLE LESSON:

Reach out to someone who is going through a difficult time and offer them words of encouragement and support. Share your own experiences of overcoming adversity and remind them of God's love and faithfulness. Remember, even in our darkest moments, God's light shines brightest. He offers us both healing and strength to get through it.

Thank You for Reading

About the Author

Monique L. Ross is the mother of three beautiful daughters and one son, and grandmother of three. After serving as a military wife for 21 years, she is now a widow living in Jacksonville, Florida. While leading her community as a philanthropist and founder of LMonique Foundation, she is also a committed life coach, author, and youth advocate.

Visit https://tcrich.org/ for more.

Find us on Facebook:
The Carter Ross Institute of Healing and Change

And on Instagram:
@carterrossinstitute

www.ingramcontent.com/pod-product-compliance
Lightning Source LLC
Chambersburg PA
CBHW050044080526
44586CB00014B/1441